. . . IF YOU LIVED WITH
the Cherokee

by Peter and Connie Roop
illustrated by Kevin Smith

SCHOLASTIC INC.

New York London Toronto Auckland Sydney

CONTENTS

Introduction

Native Americans were the first people to live in what we now call the United States. By 1776, when the United States became a nation, there were about 250 different Native American tribes scattered across the land.

Each tribe had its own customs and way of life. The type of food the people ate and the kind of houses they built depended on the climate and the wildlife of the area where they lived. Each tribe had its own language, its own style of clothes, its own religion, its own games.

This book tells about how the Cherokee people lived long ago, from the year 1740 (thirty-six years before the United States became a nation) until 1838. During those years, the Cherokee hunted, farmed, made war, and traded throughout the Great Smoky Mountains in America's Southeast. At the end of the book, you will read about the Cherokee today.

The green section on the map of the United States shows where the Cherokee lived.

Who are the Cherokee?

The Cherokee call themselves *Aniyunwiya*, meaning "the Principal People." Long ago, they came from the Northeast, home of the Iroquois-speaking tribes—the Huron, Seneca, Cayuga, Oneida, Onondaga, and Mohawk Nations. When the Cherokee migrated south to the Great Smoky Mountains, they kept the language of their ancestors.

For over a thousand years, the Cherokee enjoyed their mountain homeland. They believed it was the center of the world. They pictured it as an island hanging by four cords from the sky.

Then men from across the ocean came to the Cherokee land. An explorer from Spain named Hernando de Soto was the first person from Europe to meet the Cherokee. That was in the year 1540. De Soto and his men were looking for gold in the mountains. Later, people from England and France came to settle in the area. Cherokee life changed as the Native Americans began to trade with the new settlers.

What was it like to be a Cherokee 200 years ago? What would your home be like? Would you get to play? What clothes would you wear? This book will tell you what it would be like if you lived with the Cherokee.

Look at the time line. The part in color shows the years this book is about.

1620	1740	1776–1781	1787	1809	1812	1829	1837	1861
Pilgrims land at Plymouth Rock		American Revolution/ 13 colonies become United States		Abraham Lincoln is born		Andrew Jackson elected 7th President		Abraham Lincoln elected 16th President
			United States Constitution is written		War of 1812		Martin Van Buren elected 8th President	

What would you look like?

If you were Cherokee, the color of your skin might be light tan to dark tan. Your hair would be black and straight. You would be slim because of the games you played and the work you did.

If you were a girl, you rarely cut your hair. For the Cherokee, long hair was beautiful hair. When your hair was long enough, you tied it up.

Boys and men shaved or plucked their hair so that only a small patch was left on top.

What did you wear?

Before the new settlers came, your clothes were made from animal skins.

In summer, children under the age of eight didn't have to worry about clothes — they wore nothing in the warm months.

Men and older boys wore deerskin shirts and breech-clouts. A breechclout was a band of deerskin that hung from a belt at the waist. Women and older girls wore deerskin skirts wrapped around their waists.

In winter, men and boys wore animal skins, such as bear, panther, and beaver, with the fur on the inside for warmth. They wore moccasins on their feet and long deerskin leggings. Women and girls wore skirts made of buffalo calfskin, with the hair on the inside. They wore deerskin shirts decorated with small turkey feathers.

Women and girls wore jewelry around their necks, wrists, and ankles. You made your own jewelry from shells, seeds, bone, animal teeth, stones, and feathers. Men liked to wear armbands of leather or copper, and hair decorations, such as feathers.

Cherokee people also used shell beads, stone disks, porcupine quills, feathers, and animal hair to decorate their clothes.

Cherokee clothes changed when the Cherokee began trading with new white settlers. Shirts and skirts were made from cloth instead of animal skins. Glass beads from Spain and France were used to decorate clothing.

Who was in your family?

You would live with your mother and father and brothers and sisters and your mother's parents, but you would belong to an even larger family called a clan.

There were seven clans — Bird, Wolf, Deer, Wild Potato, Long Hair, Blue, and Paint. Members of each clan lived in every village.

Your mother and father belonged to different clans. You would be part of your mother's clan, not your father's. If your mother was a Bird and your father a Paint, you would be a Bird. Your relatives were your mother's family: her mother, grandmother, aunts, sisters, brothers and cousins.

How did people get married?

To get married, your two families exchanged special gifts. The groom would send deer meat to the girl's family. This proved he was a good hunter and would always provide his wife with food. The bride gave him an ear of corn to show she would tend to her gardening and she could prepare good food.

After the wedding ceremony, the man moved into the woman's house with her family.

To get divorced, a Cherokee woman had only to put her husband's things outside the door of their house. That meant he had to move away.

It was forbidden to marry someone from your own clan.

How did you get your name?

You might have several different names during your life. First, your parents named you. Four to seven days after your birth, your family held a special ceremony. That was when you got your name. You might be named for something special, such as your eyes or your smile.

When you were older, you could add a name or change your name. You might pick your new name to show something important you could do. Or you might choose a name to show how you did something difficult or dangerous or to describe something about you.

If you were a good swimmer, you might wish to be named *Ayunini*, which means Swimmer. If you were a happy person, you might wish to be called *Ahyoka*: She Who Brings Happiness. If you were beautiful, you might want to be named *Kamama*: Butterfly. A good hunter might choose the name *Kanati*: Lucky Hunter.

As you grew older you could change your name again.

What would your house be like?

You would live in two different houses with your large family. One house would be your home in the hot summer months. Your winter home would be nearby.

Your summer home might be made entirely of logs. Or it might be made of small trees and stalks of switch grass, tall, bamboo-like cane grass that grew near the river. Posts cut from trees made the frame of the house and stalks of dry cane were woven between the posts to make the walls. The cane was then covered with a thin layer of mud.

The door of your summer house was a deerskin that could be pulled back to let in sunlight and cool breezes. There was a roof made of tree bark shingles, with a hole to let out smoke from the fireplace that was in the center of the house.

Your bed would be at one end along with your family's beds. The bed frames were made of woven cane stalks held up by wooden posts. Pine boughs or moss were placed under a woven grass mat for soft bedding like a mattress. Beaver, otter, or buffalo skin blankets kept you warm.

Your father's weapons would hang from a wall within easy reach should enemies attack. There would be plenty of room in your summer house for you to weave baskets, repair weapons, or make new deerskin clothes.

Near your two homes would be a small cone-shaped building on tall stilt legs. Corn for planting and eating would be stored in this house. The stilt legs would keep rodents and other animals from stealing your family's precious corn.

Your winter house, or *asi*, was round and had a thatched roof made of reeds shaped like a cone. Your *asi* had no windows. To enter, you crawled through a small round door. The thick mud walls kept the winter cold out and the heat in.

A fire always burned on the hearth in the center of your winter home. Inside the *asi* you would be warm all winter as you listened to stories, mended clothes, or played guessing games.

Your family's household would be one of dozens in a Cherokee village.

What was a Cherokee village like?

Your village might have 200 to 400 or more people living in it. The village would be one of the sixty to eighty villages stretching along rivers in Cherokee country.

The rivers gave you fish to eat and freshwater for drinking and bathing, and the cane used to make buildings and many things you needed, such as beds, baskets, and fishing traps. The rivers were also the roads on which you would canoe to visit another Cherokee village.

The council house stood in the center of your village. It was the most important building. In some villages the council house was built atop a high mound of earth. The council house was made of woven cane covered with a layer of mud, just like your summer home.

A sacred fire always burned in the council house. Seven different kinds of wood were used in the fire. The seats behind the fire were for the tribal leaders. The rest of the tribe sat on their separate clan benches.

A big council house could hold more than 400 Cherokee as they watched dances and held meetings or religious ceremonies.

Next to the council house was a large open square, with seven arbors along the sides, one for each clan. The arbors were made of four posts topped by a slanted roof covered with leaves. From your arbor, the members of your clan could watch the dances, games, and ceremonies held on the square.

The summer and winter family houses were built beyond the square, but not far away. According to Cherokee tradition, a home should be close enough for you to hear a drum beaten on the square.

Your mother would have a small family garden near your house, but most of the corn you ate was grown in the big village cornfield. The field would be in a valley with rich soil and lots of water. All of the women and girls helped take care of this cornfield.

The fields and forests surrounding your village were free for anyone to hunt in or explore.

Many Cherokee villages had a tall wall of pointed wooden posts surrounding them. This wall helped keep wild animals and enemies out of the village.

Who were the village leaders?

Each village had two chiefs, one for peace and one for war. The White Chief, or Peace Chief, helped with religious ceremonies. He also made sure people got along. He dressed in white deerskins to show who he was. He was a man known for his bravery and wisdom. He had seven men who helped him rule, one from each clan.

The War Chief, or Red Chief, was in charge only in times of war. He wore red clothes. He was selected as War Chief because of his skills as a leader and a warrior. He also had seven clan members to help him.

A group of War Women, or Beloved Women, was at every war council. War Women had won honors in fighting wars or had warrior sons. The War Women helped the Red Chief plan when to attack an enemy.

There were other important people in your tribe. The headmen helped the chiefs make decisions, make laws, and conduct religious ceremonies. A priest was also an important religious leader of the tribe. The priest often talked for hours about the correct spiritual way to live. When he finished everyone said, "Toeuhah," which means "It is true."

A woman could not be a chief, but she had the same rights as a man.

What jobs did you do?

Everyone helped in whatever way they could. No matter what your age, you helped your family and your village.

If you were a girl, you would help the women plant and harvest the village's corn.

You would help your mother in your family's garden.

Your mother would teach you which mushrooms, berries, and nuts were safe to pick.

You would take care of the tobacco grown for religious ceremonies.

You would help build your summer and winter homes.

You would cook, make baskets and clay pots, and care for younger children.

Your days would be very busy indeed as you learned the skills you would need to become a successful mother and the leader of a family.

A boy's day would be busy, too, as he learned the skills needed to make him a strong Cherokee warrior.

Boys would be taught by their mother's brother to hunt and fish, and to make bows and arrows, arrowheads, and blowguns. They would cut down trees for house-building.

They would help make canoes.

The Cherokee rarely punished their children if they misbehaved. They did not spank a child. Children who acted up might be made fun of and teased until they were better behaved. Or they might simply be ignored — no one would talk to them, play with them, or be with them until the punishment was over.

What tools would you use?

Before the new settlers from England and Europe came to America, your tools would have been stones and bones.

Boys would use a sharp rock to smooth wood for bows and arrows. Arrowheads were chipped from a hard stone called flint using the tip of a deer antler. Blowguns were made from cane. Stone axes were used to cut down trees. Bones and bent sticks made good fishhooks.

Girls used sharp stones to cut tall cane stalks into long, thin pieces. They would then strip off the thin outer "skin" and weave the strips into baskets or mats. The mats, used at home or in religious ceremonies, were dyed with colors made from berries, nuts, and roots.

A girl also might make her own hoe for the garden by tying a flat stone onto a stick with a strip of leather. They used bone needles for sewing clothes.

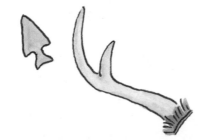

When the new settlers came, the Cherokee stopped using stone and bone tools. Instead, they traded animal skins for sharp steel axes, steel hoes, iron cooking kettles, metal fishhooks, and steel sewing needles.

What did you eat?

There was plenty to eat in Cherokee country, and you could eat whenever you were hungry. There were no regular mealtimes.

Depending on the time of year, you would have plums, grapes, berries, mushrooms, wild greens, persimmons, nuts, and wild potatoes.

Corn was a favorite meal, cooked in soups and stews, and ground into meal to make bread. Beans, pumpkins, squash, and sunflower seeds from your garden would also taste good. You could add honey or maple sap boiled into syrup to sweeten your food.

Meat came from the animals of the forests, meadows, and streams: deer, bear, elk, buffalo, squirrels, birds, frogs, fish, mussels, and crayfish.

How did you hunt and fish?

Hunting was the work of men and boys. They used bows and arrows to hunt large game, such as deer. Sometimes they used spears. Blowguns and darts were used to hunt smaller animals — rabbits, groundhogs, squirrels, and birds. Before a Cherokee boy could use a bow and arrow, he first had to prove his skill with the blowgun.

Fishing was another important skill. You might use bone hooks or box traps made of cane to catch trout, catfish, and other fish.

There was even a way to get fish without using a hook or trap. First, a dam would be built across a stream. Then horse-chestnut juice would be put into the water. The juice put the fish to sleep. You would wade in and pick out just the fish you needed. Then the dam was knocked down. The running water woke up the remaining fish, which swam away.

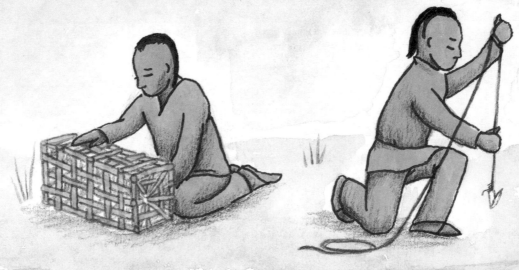

Were there special hunting ceremonies?

Yes. When hunters were going off on a big hunt, the whole village took part in animal dances. These dances were held to make certain that the hunt would be successful.

There were different dances for different animals. The Beaver Dance and the Raccoon Dance acted out the hunting, killing, and skinning of these animals. The Buffalo Hunt Dance was performed by men and women acting like bull and cow buffaloes. The Bear Dance was a fall favorite. The Cherokee believed bears had once been human and were the eighth Cherokee clan.

Because of the Cherokee belief that animals had their own spirits, it was important to show respect for their lives. Before a man could hunt, he had to pray to the animal spirits and ask permission to take their lives. If there was trouble with the hunt, the people believed something had gone wrong with their ceremonies and prayers.

In the early times, Cherokee men hunted only for the food and skins they needed to survive. After the new settlers came, they hunted more beaver, more bear, and more deer for skins to trade. Animal skins were in such great demand that in one year the Cherokee traded over a million deerskins.

How did you make a canoe?

You needed a canoe to fish or travel on the many rivers. You would use a dugout canoe. A dugout was a canoe made from one long log. The best wood was poplar or pine.

First, the tree would be cut down and the trunk shaped to a point at each end. Then fire was used to hollow it out.

Dugout canoes were made in many sizes. Small canoes held two people. Large canoes could hold fifteen to twenty people. Some even held thirty-five! You would use a long pole to push against the river bottom to move your dugout. Most dugout canoes were too heavy to be carried so they were kept on the same river.

If you had no canoe and had to cross a river, you would build a raft from a bear or buffalo skin. You would tie the legs of the skin together at each end to make a raft. You would put your belongings on top. Then you would swim across the river, pushing your raft through the water.

How did you get around in the forests?

The lower mountains and valleys were crisscrossed with trails. Many of the forest trails were made by deer and other animals. Thousands of Cherokee feet made the trails smooth near the villages.

The trails connected all of the Cherokee villages. Many led to the lands of other tribes, too. Some trails were very long and ran for miles through Cherokee territory. The Great Warriors Path ran north to south through Cherokee country. The Cherokee and other tribes used the Great Warriors Path for swift raids against their enemies.

The higher mountains were very rugged and there were few trails.

Did the Cherokee ride horses?

Horses were not much use in the mountains where the Cherokee lived, so they were not as important as they were to the Sioux and other Plains Indians.

The Cherokee did have horses. People today talk about a breed called the Cherokee pony that may have been raised in Cherokee villages.

Who were your enemies?

Your greatest enemies were the neighboring Choctaw and Creek. But you might also fight the Chickasaw, Shawnee, and Seneca.

War played an important role in Cherokee life. Men and women could be warriors. It would be up to you whether to go to war or not. No one could make you fight if you did not want to.

Warriors usually went to war to seek revenge for the death of a clan member. After a war dance, you and your companions would walk single file through the woods to your enemy's village. You would call to one another with birdcalls or other animal noises. Once you had taken your enemy by surprise, you would kill only as many of the enemy as they had killed of your clan. Then you went home.

However, your enemy would want revenge and attack you again. Then you would attack in return.

To prepare for war, young Cherokee were made to endure cold, pain, and hunger. They had to listen politely while respected warriors told of their past deeds.

If you were a good warrior you might earn the title of Raven if you were a boy or Beloved Woman if you were a girl.

The Cherokee people were involved in the many wars Europeans fought for control of America. In 1754, they sided with the English against the French. In 1776, they fought with the English against the Americans in the Revolutionary War. In 1781, after the Americans won that war, the Cherokee had to give a large amount of their land to the United States.

In the War of 1812, the Cherokee helped General Andrew Jackson defeat the Creek, their longtime enemies. The Creek fought with the English against the Americans and the Cherokee in that war. Without the Cherokee at the Battle of Horseshoe Bend, General Jackson might have lost. With their help, he won. Never again would the Cherokee have to fight the Creek.

Did the Cherokee scalp their enemies?

Yes, but they did not do this before the Europeans came. They learned to scalp from the Europeans. Even then they rarely scalped an enemy.

The Cherokee used war clubs in battles. They made three kinds. One was a stick about three feet long with a large knob on the end. Another was a short club with deer antler spikes. The third was a club with a sharp rock on the end.

Brave warriors got to wear an eagle feather in their hair as a sign of courage. To earn his feather, a boy would have to be brave in battle. He would have to do a courageous or dangerous deed in front of others so they could see just how brave he was.

When the new settlers came, the Cherokee began using guns. They replaced their stone knives and clubs with steel knives and tomahawks from the Europeans.

Did you go to school?

You would not go to school in a building. But you would be learning all the time. Your parents and relatives would be your teachers.

You would learn Cherokee history by listening to the older people in your village tell stories. There were stories about how the Cherokee people were created or why a possum plays dead. They told the story of the first three Cherokee, named Kana'ti, Selu, and Wild Boy.

Other stories told of Cherokee ancestors' brave deeds. Cherokee stories were fun to hear, but they also taught lessons about good behavior and good manners.

Did you learn to read and write?

The Cherokee had no written language until 1821, when the Cherokee syllabary was created by a chief named Sequoya. A syllabary is an alphabet that is made up of sets of syllables rather than letters.

Sequoya saw that the new settlers had papers with writing on them. The papers rustled like leaves and "talked" to people through written language. He called them "talking leaves."

When he saw these talking leaves, Sequoya decided the Cherokee must have talking leaves, too. For twelve years, he worked hard making talking leaves. First, his daughter Ahyoka helped him draw hundreds of pictures, one picture of each word in Cherokee. But it was too hard to remember what every picture meant.

Then they decided to make a symbol for each Cherokee sound. They took letters from the English alphabet. They created some letters of their own. Together they made the Cherokee syllabary.

The Cherokee syllabary has eighty-five characters, one character for each sound in Cherokee. Once you learned the characters, you could write anything in the Cherokee language. Many Cherokee learned to read and write in only a few days.

Soon after Sequoya made the Cherokee syllabary, the tribe printed its own newspapers in English and Cherokee. Today, Cherokee children learn to read and write in English and in Cherokee. Some even use a computer that speaks Cherokee!

Sequoya and Ahyoka were the first people to have made up a written language all by themselves. The tall sequoia tree, the largest in America, is named in Sequoya's honor.

Here are some Cherokee words written in the symbols of the Cherokee syllabary. (All the symbols of the syllabary are shown on page 79.)

D Ꭰ is the written word *ama*, which means water.

D Ꮳ Ꮧ is the written word *atsadi*, which means fish.

Ꮟ Ꭱ Ꭲ is the written word *tlugvi*, which means tree.

Ꮝ Ꮴ Ꮹ is the written word *Sequoya*.

How did you worship?

The Cherokee were religious. You would believe in spiritual beings who created the earth, sun, moon, and stars. You believed that eagles, rattlesnakes, fire, smoke, corn, quartz crystals, the sun, the moon, and the number seven were all sacred things.

Religious priests guided the Cherokee. Priests were singled out in childhood. Twins had an especially good chance of becoming priests.

If you were picked to be a priest, your training was different from that of your friends. You would be taught how to use herbs in medicines. You learned how to use quartz crystals in sacred ceremonies. Quartz was a special rock for the Cherokee. In every council house a large quartz crystal was kept with other sacred objects.

Yowa, or the Great Spirit, was the one supreme Cherokee god. The Yowa was so sacred that only a priest could say the name out loud.

After European Christian missionaries arrived in their land, many Cherokee became Christians. The Cherokee belief in the Great Spirit made it easy for them to believe in the one Christian god.

What would you celebrate?

Festivals were held every year. These festivals celebrated important seasonal events. There were many different kinds of food. There was music and dancing. Red wooden water drums and long gourd rattles kept steady beats. Carved cane flutes played melodies. Dancers with leg rattles made of tortoise shells moved in a circle. *Shucka-shucka, shucka-shucka* went the rattles. You danced until you were too tired to go on.

The First New Moon of Spring was celebrated in March. The Green Corn Dance was in August when the young corn was ready for tasting. The Ripe Corn Ceremony was held in September when the corn was harvested.

The Friendship Ceremony, or *Atohuna*, was held in the fall. This was a time to forget grudges and to build friendships. Homes were cleaned. Old household things were burned. New clothes were made and worn-out clothes burned. Then the family fire was put out.

Atohuna was a time to begin a new year with new things and new feelings. A new sacred fire was started with coals from the old fire. Embers from this fire were carried to each home to relight the family fires.

Atohuna lasted seven days and nights. There were dances every night. Men, women, girls, and boys danced for love, friendship, and new beginnings.

A special dance, the Booger Dance, was enjoyed by everyone, especially the children. Men traded clothing with a friend and put on scary wooden masks. The masks represented enemies, evil spirits, or creatures. The men would burst into a home or the council house pretending they were enemies and do silly things that made the enemy look foolish. At other times, the men danced around a fire acting like clowns as the children tried to guess which was their father.

The Chief Dance was a festival held every seven years.

What happened if you got sick?

The Cherokee believed that sickness was caused by animals seeking revenge for the harm people did to them. They also believed that plants were the friends of people and would fight sickness. Every plant had special healing powers. The plants told the Cherokee, "I shall help man when he calls upon me in his need." This is how Cherokee medicine began.

If you got sick, your mother or grandmother would care for you. She would find special plants to make medicines to help make you feel better. The Cherokee had 400 plants they used for medicine.

If her medicines did not work, she would get the village medicine man. He would say special prayers for you to drive the sickness from your body. He would also treat you with his plant medicines.

When a person died, the body was put in a coffin and buried. The Cherokee believed your spirit went back to visit all of the places you had lived.

Seven days after a person died, a dance was held to speed the soul of the person on its way. The grave was not visited for fear it would bring bad luck.

What games did you play?

Boys enjoyed a game called hawk-fighting. To play, two boys crouched down, facing each other. Each boy put his knees under his chin, then grabbed his legs with his arms so he looked like a ball. A friend put a long stick under his knees and arms. Each player tried to tip his opponent over. The first to get tipped over was the loser.

Chunkey was another favorite game for boys. To play, a stone disk was rolled across a flat field. The players, armed with spears, chased the disk. The players threw their spears at the stone. When the stone stopped rolling, the

player whose spear was the closest got two points. You needed 100 points to win. This game was not only fun, but it taught the boys how to throw spears better.

The basket game was a favorite game for children. Six white beans and a basket were needed. Each bean had been burned on one side and left white on the other. The six beans were tossed into the air and caught in the basket. If all the beans landed with the white side up, you got three points. The basket game was enjoyed during long winter nights.

Listening to stories was a favorite activity. Your parents and grandparents would tell you funny stories and serious stories. They would tell many animal stories, such as "How the Wildcat Caught the Gobbler" or "Why the Possum's Tail Is Bare" or "How the Deer Got His Horns." They would tell tales of how the world began and how the Cherokee got fire.

Many of the stories had lessons that would help you be a better person or teach you to be a better warrior.

Stories about the Little People were taken very seriously. The Little People stood three feet tall. They spoke Cherokee and lived in the woods wherever the Cherokee lived. The Little People liked to play tricks. If an object such as a spear or a knife was found in the forest, the Cherokee believed it belonged to the Little People. It was said that if you saw a Little Person and told about it, you would die soon.

Were there any team sports?

Anesta, or stickball, was a major Cherokee sport.

Long ago, stickball games were frequently used in place of combat with an enemy. The men from two opposing tribes played the game in the square in front of their cheering families and friends. Sometimes fifty men were on a team. Using short sticks with small baskets at one end, the players tried to hurl a small deer-hide ball past their opponents' goalpost. The first team to score twelve goals won.

Stickball was rough and tumble. The opposing players hit, kicked, pushed, and sometimes even killed one another to stop points from being scored. Stickball was called "the little brother of war." The losing team frequently lost large areas of land to the winning team.

For fun, men and women, and boys and girls played a game like stickball. The females played against the males, each side trying to hit a pole with a ball. The men and boys could only throw the ball with sticks. The women and girls could use their hands to throw the ball at the goal.

Afterward, a feast and a dance celebrated the fun of this friendly game.

The modern game of lacrosse came from stickball. Today, stickball remains an important Cherokee social and religious event.

What happened to the Cherokee when the United States was formed?

After 1783, the United States government wanted the Cherokee and other tribes to live the way other Americans did. The Cherokee were supposed to become farmers, to own land, to learn to read, write, and speak English.

Many of the Cherokee did. The men learned to become farmers instead of hunters. They owned cows, pigs, horses, and sheep. They rode in wagons. Instead of cutting wood with axes, they took logs to Cherokee sawmills. They owned stores, ferries, and blacksmith shops. Some wealthy Cherokee even owned black slaves like some white farmers did.

The Cherokee women learned to spin wool instead of tanning deerskins for clothes. Cherokee children went to Christian church schools.

The Cherokee began a new kind of government. They wrote a Cherokee constitution modeled on the Constitution of the United States, which was adopted in 1781. They elected men to a national council, which made laws. They

had a Cherokee police force called the Lighthorse Guard. They created the first Native American free public school system, which all Cherokee children had to attend.

But not all Cherokee liked to see the old ways disappear. They wanted their children to remember the ways of their ancestors. Many of the Cherokee moved deeper into the mountains to avoid contact with white Americans.

What was the Trail of Tears?

In 1838, the Cherokee were told by the United States government to move west of the Mississippi to the Indian Territory, part of present-day Oklahoma. New settlers wanted more Cherokee lands, especially after gold had been discovered on them.

When the Cherokee refused to move, the United States sent 7,000 soldiers to force them out. The soldiers dragged families from their homes, not giving them time to gather their belongings. The Cherokee stood helplessly watching as new settlers took over their homes. They were then forced to live in special fenced camps where many died from the filthy conditions.

The many treaties the Cherokee signed with the United States government should have protected them. But the treaties were ignored. The Cherokee took their case to the United States Supreme Court, the highest court in America. There they won the right to keep their lands.

But then a law was passed to move the Cherokee to the Indian Territory anyway. The Cherokee had to leave their homeland.

Eight thousand Cherokee went by boat down the Tennessee River to Ohio. From the Ohio River they went down the Mississippi, and finally up the Arkansas River to Indian Territory.

The 17,000 Cherokee still left in the camps began the long march to Indian Territory. With them they carried coals from their sacred fire. Some of the men, women, and children began marching in June. The rest left in fall and winter. Some rode on horses, others in wagons. Most walked.

The Cherokee were hungry and thirsty. Many got sick and died from measles, whooping cough, and other diseases. The dead were buried in shallow graves along the trail.

Heads down, the Cherokee marched west. Through the freezing winter they marched. Few had warm clothes. Food was hard to find. Many more Cherokee died. They marched through Tennessee and Kentucky. They crossed part of Illinois. They crossed the icy Mississippi River. They kept going through Missouri and a corner of Arkansas. Finally, they reached Indian Territory.

The terrible journey lasted six months. One out of every four Cherokee who started the march did not finish it. Over 4,000 Cherokee died along the trail.

The Cherokee call the trail *Nunna-da-ul-tsun-yi*, or "the Place Where They Cried." It is also known as the Trail of Tears.

Not all of the Cherokee went west that year. Many Cherokee hid in the mountains until the soldiers were gone. There they lived much as their ancestors had: hunting, trapping, fishing, and farming. Today, they are called the Eastern Band. They live in the Qualla Boundary or Reservation in the Great Smoky Mountains of North Carolina, the heart of ancient Cherokee country.

What is it like to be a Cherokee today?

The Cherokee who reached the end of the Trail of Tears began new lives. They built new homes, farms, and schools. They built the town of Tahlequah.

Today, Tahlequah in Cherokee County, Oklahoma, is the capital of the Cherokee Nation. Here the Cherokee government meets.

The leader of the Cherokee Nation is a chief elected by the Cherokee people. The chief works with a council of fifteen members to make decisions for the Cherokee, just as councils did long ago. A woman or a man can be elected chief. In 1985, Wilma Mankiller was elected the first woman chief of the Cherokee.

Many of the streets in Tahlequah are named for Native American tribes. You can walk down Cherokee Avenue, Delaware Street, Shawnee Street, Chickasaw Street, and Choctaw Street. Many of the streets have Cherokee names, such as Keetoowah. The signs are in Cherokee and English.

There are 186,000 Cherokee living today. They are the second-largest group of Native Americans in the United States, after the Navaho. About 11,000 Cherokee, the Eastern Band, still live on a tiny part of the same land where their ancestors lived in the Great Smoky Mountains. Most Cherokee live in the Cherokee Nation in Oklahoma.

Both bands of the Cherokee have their own schools and businesses. Many Eastern Cherokee make a living using the old Cherokee skills of basketmaking, carving, and beadwork to create things to sell to tourists. Others work in local businesses or on farms. Many Western Cherokee farm or work in factories, making everything from rocket parts to cabinets.

Both bands of Cherokee are proud of their Cherokee heritage. Each has a museum telling the story of its band as well as a Cherokee village built in the same way as the villages of their ancestors. Both perform summer plays telling their history. The Eastern Cherokee perform *Unto These Hills* and the Western Cherokee perform *Trail of Tears.*

Both Cherokee bands work hard to make a good life for themselves and their children. As in days long past, they work together to take care of each other and to help one another.

In 1984, there was the first reunion of the Eastern and Western Cherokee since 1838. Thirty thousand Cherokee celebrated their traditions and culture. Coals from the sacred fire carried west along the Trail of Tears were mixed with coals from the Qualla Boundary. A new sacred fire was lit from these coals, a fire that will burn as long as the Principal People walk the earth.

THE CHEROKEE SYLLABARY

D a			**R** e	
S ga	**ꭷ** ka		**Ꮉ** ge	
Ꮵ ha			**Ꮒ** he	
W la			**ꭲ** le	
Ꮊ ma			**Ꭺ** me	
Ꮎ na	**Ꮑ** hna	**G** nah	**Ʌ** ne	
Ꮖ qua			**ꮃ** que	
Ꮜ sa	**ꭲ** s		**Ꮞ** se	
Ꮣ da	**Ꮤ** ta		**Ꮷ** de **Ꮦ** te	
Ꮬ dla	**Ꮭ** tla		**Ꮮ** tle	
Ꮹ tsa			**Ꮧ** tse	
Ꮃ wa			**ꮚ** we	
Ꮿ ya			**β** ye	

Ꭲ i	**Ꭳ** o	**Ꭴ** u	**ꭵ** v	
Ꮿ gi	**Ꭶ** go	**Ꭻ** gu	**Ꭼ** gv	
Ꭿ hi	**Ꮆ** ho	**Ꮀ** hu	**Ꮁ** hv	
Ꮅ li	**Ꮄ** lo	**Ꮄ** lu	**Ꮎ** lv	
Ꮋ mi	**Ꮙ** mo	**Ꮍ** mu		
Ꮒ ni	**Ꮓ** no	**Ꮔ** nu	**Ꮕ** nv	
Ꮖ qui	**Ꮗ** quo	**ꮙ** quu	**Ꮛ** quv	
Ꮢ si	**Ꮠ** so	**Ꮣ** su	**Ꮢ** sv	
Ꮧ di **Ꮨ** ti	**Ꮩ** do	**Ꮪ** du	**Ꮫ** dv	
Ꮳ tli	**Ꮷ** tlo	**Ꮴ** tlu	**Ꮵ** tlv	
Ꮵ tsi	**Ꮶ** tso	**Ꮷ** tsu	**Ꮸ** tsv	
Ꮼ wi	**Ꮼ** wo	**Ꮗ** wu	**Ꮽ** wv	
Ꮿ yi	**ꮀ** yo	**Ꮽ** yu	**Ᏼ** yv	

For Heidi and Sterling: Tsigeyui

ISBN 0-590-95606-X

Text copyright © 1998 by Peter and Connie Roop.
Illustrations copyright © 1998 by Scholastic Inc.
All rights reserved. Published by Scholastic Inc.
SCHOLASTIC and associated logos are trademarks
and/or registered trademarks of Scholastic Inc.

Book design by Laurie Williams

12 11 10   2 3/0

Printed in the U.S.A.
First Scholastic printing, April 1998